Migrations

Jillian Powell

Ginn

Giant Journeys

Migrating animals are amazing travellers. In a lifetime, some of them clock up enough air miles to travel to the moon and back! They migrate to find more food or better weather, or because things are getting too crowded where they are. They travel by flying, swimming, walking, hopping and slithering. Some migrate for a few months each year; for others it's a lifetime's journey. In this book you will go on a journey of your own – following some of the most spectacular mass movements on the planet!

As you track these mighty migrations, write down and keep your answers to each **QUIZ** question. (Remember, the answers are in the book!) Now, let's go travelling!

The Globetrotter

Escape the Heat!

Wildebeest Wanderer

Masai Mara

Passport Parade

WAIT FOR ME

Brave Birds

Clock up the air miles with the frequent flyers

Marathon Mammals

Tag along with the overland trekkers

It's an Eel's Life!

Get tired of travelling with the ocean drifters

DESTINATION: 1 year that way

Mighty Marines

SOUTH

Insects with Itchy Feet

Go Tracking!

Brave Birds

Birds make great travellers. They have heat-saving bodies and hollow bones that make them light. But best of all they have a built-in navigation system! Scientists believe that birds have three internal compasses, so they can tell their way by the sun, the stars and the earth's magnetic field. They also have an internal calendar that tells them when to start over-eating! Why? Well, birds build up fat reserves to get ready for a long journey.

FLYiNG FaCT

Most birds travel from north to south for better weather, but umbrella birds migrate up and down! They fly down mountains to low-altitude nests when the weather turns colder, and back up when warmer weather arrives.

In the run-up to migration, birds get excited and restless. They start to gather together and often have practice flights before the real thing! Some birds even set off on the exact same day each year.

Swallows are long-distance travellers, flying south from Europe to spend winter in southern Africa.

Name:
Arctic tern

Summer address:
The Arctic

Winter address:
The Antarctic

Occupation:
Flying

Arctic terns are world champions at migration. They breed in and around the Arctic Circle, then fly to the edge of the Antarctic ice pack during the winter. That's an amazing 21,750 miles a year – roughly once around the circumference of the Earth! After migrating south, most young Arctic terns stay in the Antarctic until they are two years old. Then they migrate back to their birthplace without the help of their parents. Scientists are still trying to work out how …

Arctic terns migrate ✳✳✳✳✳ to th

Arctic terns live in large groups called colonies. Just before they migrate, a noisy colony of Arctic terns will suddenly become quiet. Then they all take to the air together and fly away.

Boy, this is the way to travel!

Arctic terns can live for 25 years, and in that time they fly the same distance as a journey to the moon!

Marathon Mammals

They'll cross mountains, rivers and snowfields.
They'll travel thousands of miles, and face
dangers such as floods, grass fires and hungry
predators. They are the *marathon mammals*
that undertake some of the largest land
migrations on the planet. Some mammals even
follow the exact same route each year, using
paths they recognise from landmarks and scent.

When the going gets tough, the marathon mammals take to the road.

Elephants migrate when the rainy season stops and they need to find more food. They travel in family groups led by the oldest female. She knows the migration routes, and passes her knowledge down to the younger elephants. Elephants have excellent memories, and their own built-in mobile phone! As they walk, they can communicate with each other with low growling sounds, even when they are several miles apart!

Wildebeest migration is one of the most amazing spectacles on Earth. At the peak in May, more than 1.4 million wildebeest migrate from the Serengeti Plains of East Africa to the Masai Mara (and back again!). That's a round journey of over 1800 miles. The wildebeest march head to tail on their mammoth journey. On their way, they have to cross the dangerous Mara River, where crocodiles lie in wait for the stragglers. They will also face other dangers like blazing grass fires and hungry lions.

Follow the leader! Wildebeest walk or run in single file when they are on the move.

Wildebeest pick up some travelling companions on the way – like zebras and gazelles – who are also on the hunt for green grass and water as the rainy season comes to an end. Even dung beetles trail behind the wildebeest, attracted by the whiff of so much dung! More sinister are the vultures that circle overhead – keeping watch for the sick, injured or tired animals that could provide an easy meal.

FaST-MoViNG FaCT

Wildebeest are one of the fastest animals on land – running at up to 50 miles per hour. And it comes naturally to them – wildebeest calves can stand and run a few minutes after they are born!

Each spring, huge herds of caribou migrate hundreds of miles across snowy mountains, flooded rivers and lakes. They spend the summer months grazing on the lush grasses along the Arctic coast. The growing calves have plenty of food and are safe from predators and biting insects. But as the coast gets colder and windier, the herd starts heading back to Alaska.

Name:
Caribou

Summer address:
The Arctic coast

Winter address:
Alaska and the Yukon Territory

Occupation:
Walking AND swimming

On their long journey, the caribou have to cross the mighty Porcupine River. They have hollow hairs that act like a built-in life jacket, helping to keep them afloat in the deep water. The hairs also trap any heat to keep them warm in winter. Even their hooves are adapted for the journey, acting like snowshoes to help them grip on ice and snow.

Some herds contain up to 123,000 caribou, travelling together like a river over the landscape.

It's an Eel's Life!

1

An eel has an easy start to life. It drifts along as a larva on the Gulf Stream in the Atlantic Ocean. For three years, the larva can take it easy …

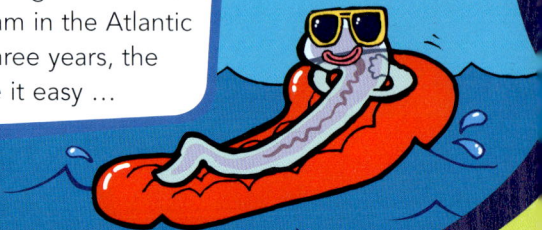

HOME SWEET HOME

The eel finally makes it home, to where it was born. Here it breeds … and then dies!

4

2

The larva grows into a tiny eel, and now comes the hard bit. It has reached an estuary in Europe and needs to swim upstream. Up waterfalls, across dams and even over land, the eel swims to reach inland waters …

3

The eel is now an adult, and guess what? It's now got to start swimming all the way back to the Atlantic Ocean! The eel travels for a year and a half, swimming during the night for safety …

Mighty Marines

These amazing sea creatures can swim great distances – sometimes across a whole ocean. Even a herring can migrate nearly 2000 miles – that's not bad for a fish just 30 centimetres long! Many migrating marine animals use the same routes each year, often following a coastline. Fish can sense the electric fields generated by water movements – so they use water currents and wind direction to guide them.

And they're off! Baby sea turtles begin their mad scramble to reach the sea.

Baby sea turtles are hardly out of their underground nests when they begin their fantastic journey. Somehow, they'll find their way across the Atlantic Ocean and back – a mighty migration of 9000 miles! Scientists think that the tiny turtles crawl across the sand heading for the bright horizon. Then they swim into the waves to get out to sea. Once in deeper water, the turtles can read the Earth's magnetic field to navigate across the ocean.

Whales migrate further than any other animal. In the summer, they eat as much as they can to build up their blubber and fat reserves. Then, as the winter approaches, they migrate to warmer seas. They swim almost constantly, surviving on their body fat – sometimes going without food for up to five months!

FREE-LIFT FACT

ATLANTIC OCEAN

A grey whale can have up to 200 kilograms of barnacles hitchhiking a ride on its head and body!

A humpback having a whale of a time on its long journey

21

Name:
Pacific salmon

Birthplace:
Freshwater river

Occupation:
Swimming and
high jumping

Salmon hatch from eggs in freshwater rivers and streams. As young fish, they begin swimming down the rivers and out to sea, where they live for up to four years. It's then time to begin the marathon journey back to their birthplace. Their homing instinct is so strong, they can pinpoint the mouth of their birth-stream in a huge ocean! After a long, hard journey, the salmon arrive back to where they were born to breed, lay eggs, and die!

Salmon need to survive predators such as

Salmon use their super sense of smell on their amazing journey: they can recognise a single drop of their home stream water, mixed in 1000 litres of other water! On their way, salmon change colour to suit the river or the sea, and even burn their own muscles to give them energy.

Salmon face many hazards during their migration, from ravenous sharks and bears to towering waterfalls.

Insects with Itchy Feet

They're only small but they can fly across whole continents and oceans. These insects with itchy feet take to their wings to escape bad weather and find better homes and more food. Some hitch a ride on winds and take it easy; one type of grasshopper flies straight up in the sky until it reaches the ideal wind currents to carry it to its summer feeding ground.

FReQueNT-TRaVeLLeR FaCT

The palolo worm is a regular traveller. It migrates every month, taking its cue from its own alarm clock – the moon!

Insects that need to navigate long journeys fly high enough to rise above air currents that could force them off course. Monarch butterflies have been spotted by glider pilots flying at heights of 1200 metres!

Name:
Monarch butterfly

Occupation:
Following the sun!

Travel visas:
Mexico, Florida,
Southern California

Every year, millions of North American Monarch butterflies fly south as the weather turns colder. They travel to California, or Florida, or the mountain forests of Mexico. To keep them going, the butterflies store fat in their abdomens, and stop to drink nectar from flowers to give them energy for their long-distance flight. They even have their own built-in protection against predators like birds that might gobble them up as they fly south. They feed on milkweed, which contains toxins, so they are a poisonous mouthful!

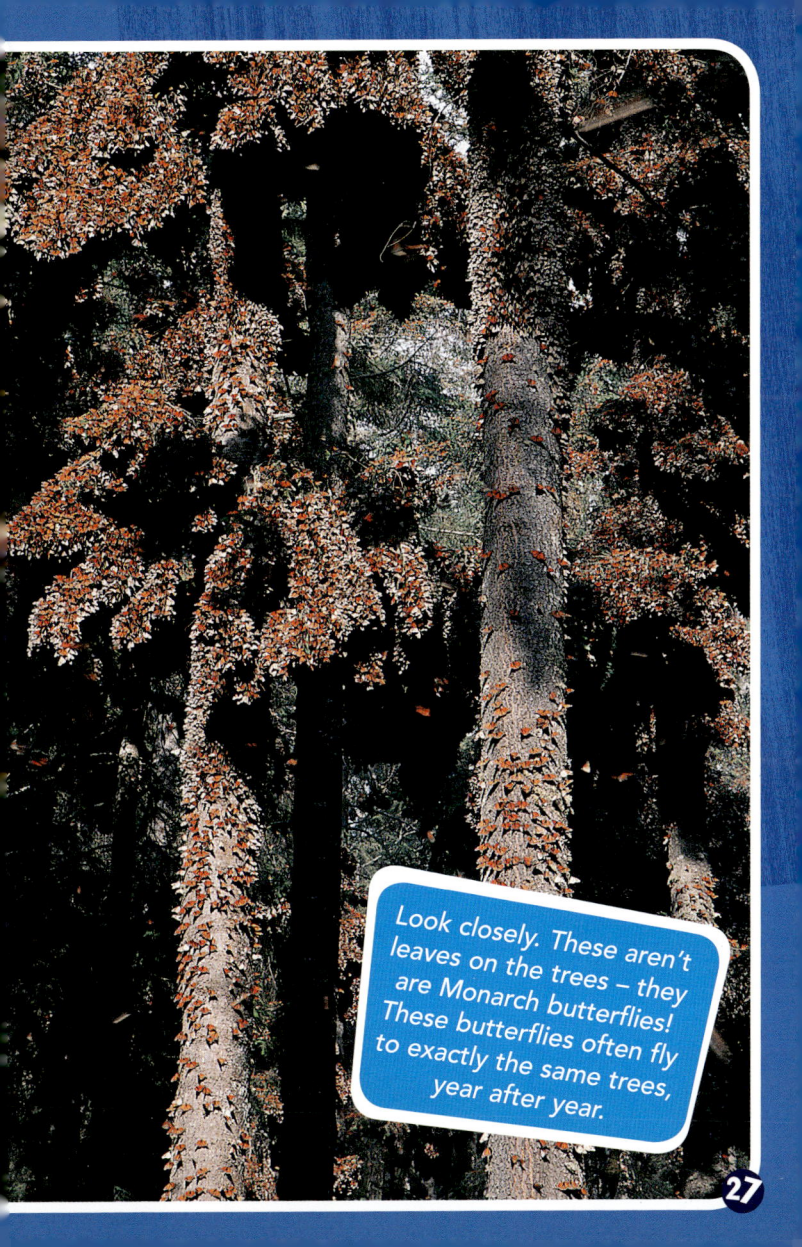

Look closely. These aren't leaves on the trees – they are Monarch butterflies! These butterflies often fly to exactly the same trees, year after year.

Locusts don't often migrate, but when they do, they do it in style! Hot weather and crowding can trigger locusts to swarm and migrate. But you don't want to be around when a swarm comes to town. Why? Well, they can destroy acres of crops and trees within minutes. **Locusts can even turn day into night!**

The longest insect migration ever was by desert locusts in 1988. They migrated 2800 miles from Africa, across the Atlantic Ocean to the West Indies.

Predators don't like to eat Monarch butterfli

A swarm of locusts can block out the sun!

Go Tracking!

The amazing journeys of migrating animals can be tracked by scientists using everything from simple tags and leg bands to the latest radar and radio technology. Tiny lightweight tags can be fitted to birds' legs and insects' wings, and radio transmitters can be attached to whales, turtles and other sea creatures.

FITTING FACT

Radio transmitters are carried in a harness, which is strapped to an animal's body. The harness is specially designed for each animal species, to make sure it fits perfectly and is comfortable.

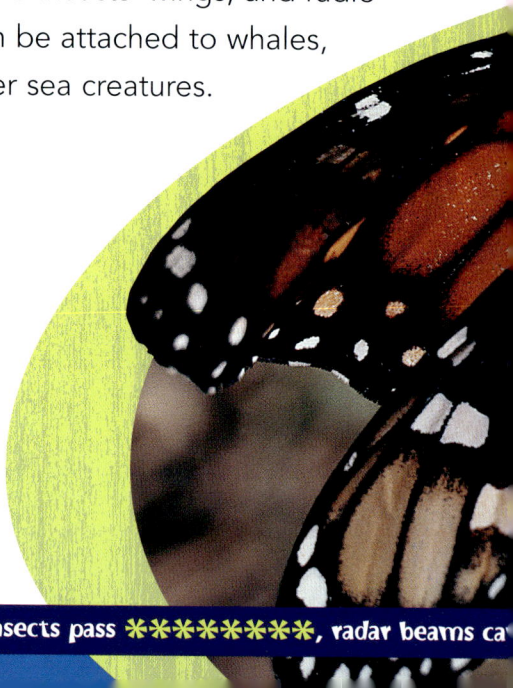

As insects pass ✳✳✳✳✳✳✳✳✳, radar beams ca

Radar beams can detect migrating insects as they pass overhead – useful when there's a swarm of locusts heading your way! Scientists also use satellite trackers to help them monitor and protect endangered birds and animals. By tracking migration patterns, scientists can even learn more about global warming.

ENVIE A
ZOOLOGI
UNIVERSIT
TORONTO
CANADA

Tags can be fitted to even the smallest of animals. Scientists will be able to track this Monarch butterfly's next mighty migration.

So there's some truly terrific travellers for you! Did you get the answers to all the quiz questions? Now, juggle with the first letters of all the answers to make a word that describes something we might need when we go travelling – but these animals already have on board!

Calves

Sharks

Poisonous

Antarctic

Mouthful

South

Overhead

Juggle with the first letters SACSPMO and you get COMPASS – something these amazing travellers have in their brains!